SOUTH AFRICA
AT THE CROSSROADS

Jacqueline Drobis Meisel

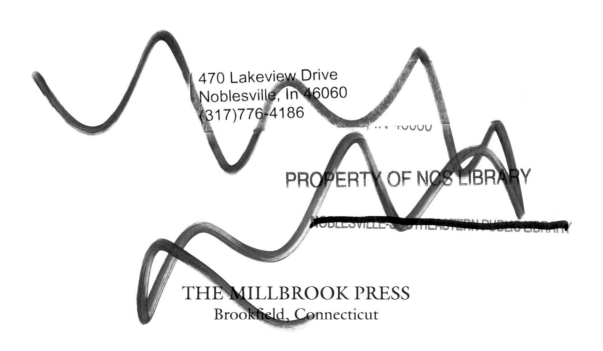

THE MILLBROOK PRESS
Brookfield, Connecticut

Published by The Millbrook Press
2 Old New Milford Road
Brookfield, CT 06804
© 1994 Blackbirch Graphics, Inc.

5 4 3 2 1

Created and produced in association with Blackbirch Graphics.
Series Editor: Tanya Lee Stone

Library of Congress Cataloging-in-Publication Data
Meisel, Jacqueline.
    South Africa at the crossroads / by Jacqueline Drobis Meisel.
      p.   cm. — (Headliners)
    Includes bibliographical references and index.
      1. South Africa—Politics and government—1989–   —Juvenile literature.
2. Apartheid—South Africa—Juvenile literature. 3. Elections—South Africa—
Juvenile literature. [1. South Africa—Politics and government. 2. Apartheid—South Africa.] I. Title. II. Series.
    ISBN 1-56294-511-4 (lib. bdg.)
    DT1970.M54 1994
    968.06'4—dc20
                                                94-8350
                                                    CIP
                                                      AC

Contents

Chapter 1

A Nation at the Crossroads

A school bus slips out of the stream of rush hour traffic and pulls over to let some children off at their stop. Up ahead at an intersection stands a newspaper vendor holding up a copy of the *Daily News.* Passing motorists can read the headline:

"South Africa's First Free Democratic Election Scheduled for 1994!"

The black bus driver points out the headline to his young passengers. They are kids of all races whose junior high school has recently been integrated. Shouts of amazement and joy shake the bus. This will be the first time that all citizens, regardless of color, will be allowed to vote.

A white businessman driving a sports car stops at a red light. He honks his horn to get the attention of the newspaper seller. Opening his window, he passes some money through the crack and takes his paper. He glances at the headline with a worried frown. The light turns green and he drives away.

All over South Africa people reacted to the announcement of the 1994 elections with a mixture of excitement and nervousness. At the news, the eyes of the world turned both anxiously and hopefully on this nation at the

> South Africa is
> about to enter
> a new age of
> democracy

Opposite:
Black and white students enjoy the advantages of integration at a Johannesburg school.

SLEGS BLANKES
EUROPEANS ONLY

A group of black South Africans boarded a restricted "Europeans Only" train compartment in 1952 to protest the rigid segregation and strict racial policies of apartheid. Since it officially began in 1948, apartheid spawned many political groups who were both in favor of and against the practice.

southern tip of the African continent. Everyone wondered if the elections would lead to democracy in South Africa.

In the years leading up to the elections, South Africa was seen as a deeply *un*democratic country, by people around the world as well as by most of its own citizens. This was due largely to its government's policy of apartheid. Apartheid literally means "separateness" and the laws the government enacted as a result of this policy separated its black and white people. Not only did apartheid divide the society along racial lines, but it strictly regulated the daily lives of blacks—the majority of South Africa's population—while assuring whites a superior status. In resistance, anti-apartheid groups formed. Sometimes they protested peacefully. Other times they clashed violently with police and armed forces. South Africans asked: Would the elections finally end apartheid and the unrest it had caused?

The rest of the world, long critical of apartheid, watched and waited to see how this transition to democracy would be handled. The international community also understood that these elections represented an important turning point in the balance of power in southern Africa, and for all the people who lived there. There was, however, no guarantee of a peaceful shift of power from the hands of the white minority to a government that represents all South Africans.

SOUTH AFRICA

Key

- ◎ National Capital
- • Okiep City
- — International Boundary
- — Province Boundary
- *Cape* Province Name

AFRICA

Area of Detail

Life Under the Laws

How did apartheid come to play so important a role in South Africa's—and the world's—affairs? The policy was instituted when the National Party (NP) came to power in 1948 with D. F. Malan as prime minister. Whites were greatly outnumbered by blacks, who made up 88 percent of the population, and were afraid of losing their political power and privilege. Malan's successful election campaign was based on the principles of apartheid.

Once in office, Malan and his party passed laws supporting apartheid. One of the most important laws was the Group Areas Act of 1949, under which each race had its own designated area where only it could live. The other was the Population Registration Act of 1950, which defined categories of "race" to which each person belonged—white, black, colored (mixed race), or Asiatic/Indian. (Both of these acts have since been repealed.) In time, a complex system of segregation was firmly in place and a crucial right, that of being allowed to vote, was reserved only for whites.

When D. F. Malan (shown here with his wife) became South Africa's prime minister in 1948, the policies of apartheid were formally instituted.

A Johannesburg resident shows his official Pass Book. Under apartheid, every black person needed this document to enter white areas.

Under apartheid, mixed marriages were also prohibited. As part of the elaborate laws that forced people to remain in their own areas, a black person had to carry a Pass Book at all times. This document authorized him or her to be in white urban areas only if employed there. If a Pass Book was not current, he or she would be jailed and fined, and sometimes sent back to his or her homeland or separate tribal area. Over the years, blacks were also removed from their homes and forced to live in areas reserved for them by the government.

Laws also required that blacks and whites take separate buses to different schools. Apartheid also enforced the segregation of elevators, public restrooms, movie theaters, beaches, and restaurants. The effect of apartheid was so

A Mutual Need

No one political party could claim to represent all black South Africans, however, the ANC came the closest. Nelson Mandela was seen by many—both within South Africa and in the international community—as the voice of reason in the midst of chaos. Although imprisoned for twenty-six years, he was never forgotten by South Africans who wanted to see apartheid abolished. He was tried along with other militant members of the ANC for attempting to violently overthrow the government, and convicted in 1964. He served most of his sentence on desolate Robben Island off the coast of South Africa near Cape Town, but continued to be revered as a leader for the duration of his imprisonment. He was released by President F. W. de Klerk, who lifted the ban on the ANC in 1990. The ANC demonstrated a willingness to negotiate. It realized that it had to be flexible if there was to be a peaceful transition to democracy, and agreed to help create a democratic multi-party government.

President de Klerk was leader of the National Party, originally the ideological opposite of the ANC. He steered his country through extremely difficult times. He was willing to make some concessions along the way, without losing sight of his ultimate goal—a new, democratic South Africa. He realized that it was only through being flexible that he would be able to secure the rights and safety of whites on the road to majority rule. His party dropped its insistence on a minority veto in exchange for a five-year power-sharing period. Conservative whites believed that the NP was giving away too much power to the blacks, while liberals felt it was "too little, too late." Still, de Klerk and the NP appeared to represent most whites who realized there was no turning back.

Mandela and de Klerk jointly accepted the Nobel Peace Prize in Norway in December 1993. These remarkable men who were once in opposite camps, through force of necessity, and the love of their country, became allies.

F. W. de Klerk, president of the National Party, and Nelson Mandela, president of the African National Congress (ANC), meet in Johannesburg for negotiations in 1992.

all-encompassing, that blacks and whites rarely got to know each other. There was seldom the opportunity to meet as peers, and language barriers made it very hard to communicate. The less blacks and whites knew about each other, the more chances there were for fear and stereotypes to grow.

A Country Divided

In sum, apartheid was institutionalized racism. It fostered hatred, resentment, and fear among South Africans, and threatened the country's future. It also outraged people around the world. That was why South Africa's vote for democracy in the 1994 election was so important.

Yet the country was not just polarized in terms of black and white. The issues in the election were far more complex. South Africa's approximately thirty million blacks originate from eight larger tribes and numerous smaller ones. They make up the political spectrum from Communists to moderates who favor a non-racist society, to more extreme black nationalists. Issues of race, class, tribal loyalties or rivalries, and religious affiliation, all affected the political choices that people made in the election.

South Africa's approximately five million whites are also far from united. They, too, represent a wide spectrum of political beliefs. There are white anti-apartheid activists who have built schools and clinics in the black townships, and white supremacists who would rather secede from the republic than be a part of integrating it.

The best-known names and parties at the time of the elections were those of President F. W. de Klerk, leader of the National Party, and Nelson Mandela, president of the African National Congress (ANC). These two men and their parties have undergone many changes: Mandela was the leader of a group that advocated armed resistance to apartheid, and de Klerk held pro-apartheid views. Eventually, Mandela made a public announcement that he would stop armed protests and de Klerk renounced his support of most of the apartheid rules. In fact, most South Africans and international leaders pinned their hopes on these men working together. Mandela and de Klerk seemed to realize that there could be no other possible peaceful solution for South Africa than for old enemies to join hands.

Another key player in the South African drama was Zulu Chief Mangosuthu Gatsha Buthelezi and his armed Inkatha Freedom Party (IFP). Buthelezi was committed to the total eradication of apartheid. He believed that free enterprise, privately owned business, would be the economic system that would best serve the interests of the masses. Buthelezi's interest in free enterprise led him to an alliance with the white government. Because of this alliance, and the fact that Buthelezi and IFP were threatened by the prospect of a government dominated by the ANC, there was a history of violence between the ANC and IFP. (In 1991, it was revealed that the government funded some of Inkatha's anti-ANC activities. Some of the worst black-on-black violence has been between these two groups.) Many believe that the likelihood of an ANC victory in the elections drove Buthelezi's party to withdraw temporarily from the elections in February 1994.

Among the more extreme black nationalist groups was the Pan Africanist Congress (PAC) led by Clarence Makwetu. Basically, its ideology was "Africa for Africans" and its armed wing was the Azanian People's Liberation Army (APLA). Whites were not eligible for membership, and were seen as unwelcome settlers in South Africa. The APLA slogan was, "One settler, one bullet." APLA claimed responsibility for a number of acts of violence against white civilians, including a killing that took place near one of South Africa's major cities, Cape Town, in 1993 of visiting American student, Amy Biehl. Ironically, Biehl was in South Africa to help fight for black rights. Her death was an example of a random act of anti-white violence.

Before the elections in 1994, Zach de Beer led the Democratic party, which wanted a new government based on human rights and non-racist principles.

Most white extremist groups were represented by the Afrikaner-Volksunie. Some of the parties belonging to the Volksunie were the Afrikaner Weerstandsbeweging, or Afrikaner Resistance Movement (AWB), the Conservative party, and the Herstigte Nasionale Party, or Reconstituted National Party (HNP). This alliance advocated a policy of partition whereby each race would have its own area of jurisdiction within a federation. For itself it sought a self-governing state to be called Oranje.

There were numerous other parties and factions, including the Democratic party led by Zach de Beer. The Democratic party sought a negotiated, fully democratic, non-racist constitution based on human rights and the rule of law in which all citizens would have an equal voice.

From these various parties South Africans had to choose leaders who could put the country on the road toward equality. Yet everyone knew this would be a difficult task, given the racial divisions of South Africa's history.

14

Chapter 2

Europe Meets Africa: South Africa to 1948

In order to understand the exciting events of 1994, it is necessary to take a closer look at the history that has led up to the dawn of democracy in South Africa. As a result of apartheid, at least three generations of South African schoolchildren have been taught that South African history began in 1652, with the arrival of the first Dutch settlers. Up until the early 1990s, textbooks and teachers were required to echo the South African Department of Education's official version of history: When the Europeans arrived, large parts of South Africa were uninhabited and could be freely acquired.

As a result of this way of teaching, black students did not learn about their heritage, and white students were offered an inaccurate version of theirs. Today, scholars are rediscovering a more accurate history.

> Since 1652, South Africa has struggled with European invaders who looked to exploit the land and its people

Before and After the Europeans Arrived

For many thousands of years, southern Africa was inhabited by small groups of people known as the San. About two thousand years ago, sheep, goat, and cattle herders related to the San first appeared in South Africa. These were the Khoikhoi (pronounced KOY-KOY).

Recent research indicates that there were other societies in southern Africa as early as AD 300. A number of later societies began with Bantu-speaking immigrants who

Opposite:
European employees of the Republic Gold Company pose in front of a mine entrance in De Kaap with their South African workers in 1888.

arrived from the north around AD 1200. Their use of tools led to improved agricultural techniques and they established relatively settled communities. These Bantu-speaking people lived in round huts linked by walls to keep livestock inside and predators outside.

The first Europeans encountered by the Khoikhoi were Portuguese sailors in the 1400s, who occasionally bartered with them for food. However, it was Dutch agents of the Dutch East India Company who put down roots in what is today known as South Africa. The Dutch East India Company imported products such as silk and spices from the East.

Many sailors grew ill on the long journey between the Netherlands and the Dutch East Indies—today's Indonesia. It was known that scurvy could be prevented by a diet that included fresh fruit and vegetables. In 1652, the company sent Jan van Riebeeck to found a refreshment station where fresh produce could be grown and sick sailors could be left to recover. The most logical location for this station was the Cape of Good Hope at the very tip of what is now South Africa.

At first, the Khoikhoi were prepared to barter with the passing ships; however, when Dutch construction of the fortified station began, there was no mistaking the whites' intention to settle in this part of the world. Their initial contacts were fairly peaceful, but over time, the situation between the Khoikhoi and the Europeans grew hostile. The Dutch were greatly disrupting the Khoikhoi way of life. Raids and rebellions erupted in an attempt by the Khoikhoi to persuade the Dutch to leave the Cape. But the Dutch had superior weaponry and were there to stay. Many Khoikhoi moved away from the Cape into other parts of southern Africa. But many others, who chose to remain, became paid servants.

The Dutch East India Company's policy was to forbid the enslavement of the original inhabitants of the Cape. However, the company was allowed to hold slaves from elsewhere. Slaves were brought from a variety of places, including West Africa, Madagascar, and the Malayan peninsula. The buying and selling of slaves continued at the Cape colony until 1834.

Although it was not the intention of the Dutch East India Company to establish a colony at the Cape, this is what the small refreshment station became. As it grew, German, Dutch, and French immigrants came to live at the Cape. The French Huguenots were Protestants who came to escape religious persecution in France. They helped develop South Africa's world class wine industry. The German settlers, on the other hand, were mostly peasant farmers who were attracted by the great mountains and fertile valleys of the Cape peninsula. These immigrants adopted the Dutch language, and eventually came to be known first as Boers, from the Dutch word for

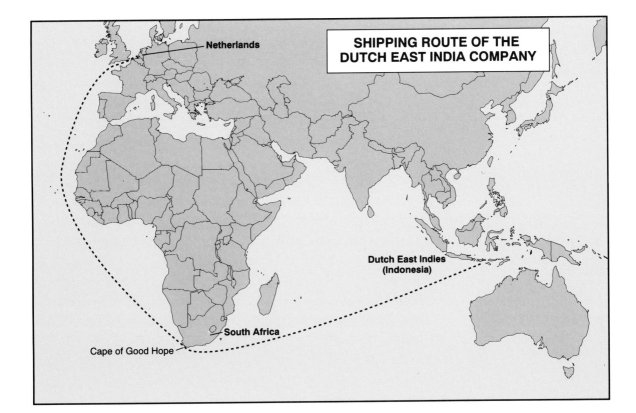

A Boer farm, typical of one found in South Africa during the 1700s. During that era, a number of Boer settlers—called trekboers— moved to the northern regions of South Africa to raise cattle.

farmers, then as Afrikaners—the white tribe. Many of these settlers populated Cape Town, a beautiful city that lies at the foot of Table Mountain.

There were other, more adventurous Boer settlers who became herders of flocks and cattle. They moved steadily north, away from "civilized" European influence and the Company's control. They were called *trekboers,* and continually moved about in search of grazing land. These Boers identified strongly with stories of the Old Testament Israelites. They saw themselves as an isolated yet chosen race, with only their God and their guns for protection. This toughness and independence can be found in their Afrikaans-speaking descendants today who still belong to the Dutch Reformed Church.

In the 1770s, eastward-moving Boers clashed with the Xhosa (pronounced KO-sa), which was a Bantu-speaking black tribe slowly migrating westward with its herds. The frontier became chaotic, with raids, skirmishes, and full-blown battles between Boers and Xhosa. When the British annexed the Cape, first from 1795 to 1802, and again in 1806, they inherited this situation.

The Great Trek

Britain was eager to acquire the Cape. It had strategic importance for trading with the East, and was an untapped market for British goods.

When the first large contingent of British settlers arrived in 1820, the white population had increased to 47,000—43,000 of whom were of Dutch extraction. However, the British emphasized literacy and education and within a short period of time, a distinctly British way of life evolved at the Cape. Both the systems of government and education were unmistakably British. Even architecture and entertainment took on a peculiarly English aspect, with Georgian square-built houses, cricket matches on the green, and the printing of English language newspapers.

Officials and missionaries arrived and settled into an uneasy relationship with white, Boer farmers who regarded this British interference with hostility. The missionaries began a liberal tradition in South Africa, encouraging peace and equality. But white farmers could not accept Khoikhois or black slaves being treated as equals.

Ultimately, all slaves in British colonies, including the Cape, were emancipated in 1833. Slave owners were paid less than half of what their slaves were really worth, and found themselves without slaves or money. The Boers, outraged by this and other interference, declared that they had enough of everything British, and moved away in 1836.

The people who packed up their covered ox wagons and headed for the interior of southern Africa, away from British control, were called the Voortrekkers, and their journey was commonly referred to as the Great Trek.

In February 1837, Piet Retief announced on behalf of all the Voortrekkers: "We quit this colony under the full assurance that the English Government has nothing more to require of us, and will allow us to govern ourselves without interference in [the] future..."

The trekkers sought to establish their own state in the interior. They had great courage and determination to embark on a dangerous journey through uncharted country. Women and children traveled in the wagons along with their possessions, while servants and animals walked behind. The men rode up in front on horseback, their guns at the ready. The Voortrekkers were very similar to the American pioneers who settled the West.

Today, some Afrikaners regard the Voortrekkers as heroes, and romanticize the Great Trek as one of the keys to white domination of South Africa.

Turn of the Century and Beyond

By 1854, southern Africa was divided into two Boer republics—the Transvaal and the Orange Free State—and two British colonies—the Cape and Natal. The discovery of diamonds, and then gold, re-activated British interest in the interior. In 1895–1896, prime minister of the Cape, Cecil John Rhodes, along with L. S. Jameson, planned and failed in an attempt to overthrow the Transvaal government of President Paul Kruger.

The failure of this raid stimulated Afrikaner nationalism through southern Africa. The English-speaking British colonies also produced a surge of nationalist feelings.

Cecil Rhodes (left) and L. S. Jameson (right) together planned to overthrow the Transvaal Boer government of Paul Kruger in 1895–1896. Their failed attempt only served to rally Boer nationalism and increase tensions between the Boers and the British.

Southern Africa was divided into two camps—pro-Boer and pro-Briton. The Transvaal and Orange Free State drew closer together and began arming for what became the Anglo-Boer War.

The Boers were vastly outnumbered by the well-equipped British. The British adopted a scorched-earth policy, in which they burned Boer crops and farmhouses, and put Boer women and children in concentration camps. Near the end of the war, the Boers resorted to guerilla tactics in this white-against-white war. Meanwhile, thousands of blacks were caught in the crossfire.

Under the provisions of the Treaty of Vereeniging signed in 1902, the two Boer republics lost their independence and became British colonies. English became the official language, although Dutch was protected in the law courts. (Afrikaans was not yet considered a "real" language, though it was widely spoken by Dutch settlers.) Britain gave the Boers financial aid for reconstruction and agreed not to give Africans the vote until after the Boers were granted self-government. The Boers (or Afrikaners, as they were now called) never intended to extend the vote to the blacks.

Lord Milner, who was made governor of all four provinces in southern Africa following the Anglo-Boer War, set about repairing the ravages of war. His plan was to encourage the immigration of English-speaking people and to anglicize the Afrikaners through education. But as Milner attempted to introduce and enforce culture, his plan failed because he caused great resentment between Afrikaners and Britons.

A National Convention met in 1908–1909 to draft a constitution. The most important decisions made were that South Africa should become a union with a bicameral—two chambered—central parliament. Each province—Cape, Natal, Transvaal, Orange Free State— would retain its own franchise, or voting qualification laws, which basically stated the property and education requirements that were necessary to vote. Qualified blacks and coloreds in the Cape had the vote, and it was entrenched in the new constitution. (This right was then repealed in 1952.)

Three African newspaper editors called a South African Native Convention in 1909 to counter the white convention that excluded blacks. They were John Jabavu, Walter Rubusana—a minister in the Congregational Church who had studied in the United States—and John Dube, who had been strongly influenced by the African-American leader Booker T. Washington. They called for the right of all adult males in all republics to vote, irrespective of color, and for an end to racial discrimination. A black delegation that traveled to England found almost no support among British politicians.

Louis Botha (left) and W. E. Gladstone (right) together headed up the Union of South Africa, which was established in 1910.

Jan Smuts (opposite top) and J. B. Hertzog (opposite bottom) worked together in 1936 to stem the growing power of the National Party, which favored British-style rule in South Africa.

The Union of South Africa—unity of the four provinces under one Parliament—came into being in 1910 under British Governor-General Lord W. E. Gladstone, with an Afrikaner prime minister, Louis Botha. The issue of black civil rights was still not addressed. In 1912, delegates at the Native Convention formed themselves into the South African Native National Congress, a powerful organization that was later called the African National Congress (ANC).

Precursors to Apartheid

Although the formal establishment of apartheid was many years away (1948), there were a great many building blocks that led up to it. The 1911 Mines and Works Act is one example. It forced blacks into the category of cheap labor, by creating and enforcing job reservation—so that only whites were eligible for higher paying jobs requiring skilled labor.

At the time of union, black rights of occupation in the different provinces were not clearly defined. The Natives Land Act of 1913 set aside approximately 10 percent of the country as reserves for blacks, who made up almost 80 percent of the population, and prevented them from owning land outside the reserves.

The 1920 Native Affairs Act was another precursor to apartheid. It paved the way for a country wide system of tribally based, but still government-appointed, district councils. The 1923 Natives (Urban Areas) Act sought to regulate the presence of Africans in the cities and towns. Local authorities were to administer Pass laws, so that only a person who had proof of employment in the town was permitted to be there. Others could be deported to the reserves.

When Britain declared war on Germany in August 1914, Prime Minister Louis Botha was asked to send soldiers to capture the German colony of South West Africa. Many Afrikaners, however, did not want to enter the war on the side of their former enemy, Britain.

Eventually the German colony of South West Africa was defeated by South African forces—both black and white—fighting for Britain. Soon after World War I ended, South West Africa was placed under South African administration with the understanding that it would one day become an independent country. Today, it is the country of Namibia.

In 1918, both Louis Botha and Jan Smuts—senior member in Botha's cabinet—attended the post-war peace conference in France and, with other world leaders, signed the Treaty of Versailles. Smuts took this as a sign that South Africa was being given some measure of independence from the British Crown and some control over its own foreign policy. J. B. Hertzog—pro-Afrikaner minister of justice in Botha's cabinet—defeated Smuts in the 1924 election to become the third prime minister of the Union of South Africa. By 1934, South Africa had achieved constitutional independence. The Union could now make its own laws. In 1936, the Native Representation Act was passed whereby blacks in the Cape were put on a separate voters roll and were allowed to elect three

Diamonds and Gold

The discovery of precious minerals dramatically changed the course of South African history. In 1867, the first diamond was found at Hopetown in an area claimed by both Boer republics, the Transvaal and the Orange Free State, which had been formed in 1854. Then, as more diamonds were discovered, the British hurried to annex land that belonged to Nicholas Waterboer, Chief of the Griqua, a black tribe from the Cape province, and declare it a British colony. This land was also in the Hopetown area and the British correctly assumed that it was rich with precious minerals.

Soon, gold was being found throughout the Transvaal, especially in the Witwatersrand, a region adjacent to Johannesburg. Big mining houses were formed by the British and white South African entrepreneurs to invest in the necessary equipment. In order to keep up with production of gold products and remain a profitable enterprise, there was a need for a cheap labor force.

The Chamber of Mines—a government department that controlled all aspects of mining—used several different methods to get workers for the mines. The government decided that taxes had to be paid in cash, not with animals such as cattle, a medium of exchange used by blacks. Thus blacks went to work in the mines to earn money so that they would be able to pay their taxes.

Africans were not the only mine workers. From Europe, including mining areas in England, came skilled miners and machine operators. No matter how low they were on the English class ladder, because they were white, they entered South African society with the guarantee of a decent standard of living.

Black workers, however, endured appalling conditions in the mines. They were separated from their families who remained in the rural areas to try to keep their farms productive. Eventually, however, as their farms became more and more impoverished, some of the women also left to try to find work in the cities. Many people eventually lived in the African "townships," ghettolike communities, that evolved on the outskirts of the white areas of town.

Living conditions were also harsh in the men's hostels on the mining compounds, and the underground work itself was dangerous and unhealthy. A Pass Book system prevented the migrant worker's family from visiting him. Even if they could reach him, there was no legal accommodation for them. In this way, the unity of the family was slowly broken down. Also, a ban on African trade unions took away any bargaining power the workers might have had to try and negotiate better wages and conditions. It was only in 1984 that the National Union of Mineworkers—an organization formed to fight for the rights of both black and white miners—was recognized.

Government-run beer halls were established on the compounds in an effort to entice workers to stay. Liquor provided them with the only escape from the drudgery of daily life. The consumption of alcohol intensified aggression, and faction fights between men of different tribes became common on the mines. Over the years, white leaders found it to their advantage to keep tribal rivalries fueled. They thought that dissatisfied workers who were fighting each other would not be inclined to unite to fight their common foe.

white members of Parliament, and blacks in the Union were represented by four whites in the Senate.

Hertzog and Smuts formed a coalition to defeat the growing National Party, which was in favor of British-style values and promoting the English language. Hardline Afrikaners were disappointed in Hertzog and broke away to form the Purified National party, which stated that it

A Bantu worker digs in a coal mine nearly two miles underground in 1947.

wanted South Africa to become a republic. (This became the party to introduce apartheid.)

In 1939, the United party split over the decision about whether South Africa should fight in World War II with Britain against Germany. Hertzog lost the critical vote in Parliament and Smuts was elected prime minister. South Africa then went to war on the side of the Allies.

STRAND & SEE
NET BLANKES
BEACH & SEA
WHITES ONLY

Chapter 3

The Years of Apartheid: 1948–1989

In 1948, the Purified National party won the whites-only elections and D. F. Malan succeeded Jan Smuts as prime minister with a platform based on apartheid. The policy of apartheid was institutionalized through a system of laws, a major goal of which was to ensure that blacks were deprived of the right to vote. (This included blacks in the Cape province who had previously been able to vote.)

From the very beginning, some groups opposed the policy. Anti-apartheid groups used a range of tactics to fight the system, from passive resistance and prayer, to bombs set off in shopping centers. The South African government devised ever more repressive methods of silencing the opposition.

From Unrest to Emergency

The South African Communist party was open to all races and opposed to apartheid. It became an illegal organization when the government passed a new law in the early 1950s, called the Suppression of Communism Act. This act gave vast powers to the minister of justice. If he thought that an individual was "furthering the aims of

> Government-sponsored racism became the official policy of South Africa in 1948

Opposite:
A black worker pushes a rubbish cart in front of a restricted beach near Cape Town.

communism," he could exclude that person from participating in public life by placing him or her under a banning order for years. A banned person could not attend any public gathering, not even a party or the movies, or be quoted in the media.

This act gave the government the power to restrict the activities of anyone it suspected of being involved in anti-apartheid activities, even if the person was not really a Communist. In the early 1950s, some of the apartheid laws were made even stricter, and the government gave itself more power to crush the opposition.

Hendrick F. Verwoerd, minister of native affairs—often called the "supreme architect" of the ideology of apartheid—introduced the Bantu Urban Authorities Act in 1951. This made it more difficult for blacks to live in white urban areas. He also made sure that the last remaining colored voters were removed from the list of eligible voters.

Other significant laws of that period prohibited mixed marriages and disallowed blacks from putting up makeshift shelters. Laws also required blacks to present Pass Books for using facilities such as public bathrooms, buses, and schools that were segregated. The government was quickly growing more totalitarian.

The ANC and the South African Indian Congress (SAIC)—a political group that formed to protect the interests of South Africans of Indian origin—decided to unite to show their opposition to apartheid and hopefully gain international recognition. When the government failed to respond, the two organizations called for a defiance campaign in 1952 that was similar to Gandhi's passive resistance campaign. In the two years of the campaign, 8,557 people were arrested for deliberately breaking apartheid laws. The campaign's main achievement was in making black people more politically conscious, and more aware of the strategy of united opposition.

A common front called the Congress Alliance was created in 1955. The ANC, the SAIC, the South African

Hendrick F. Verwoerd, who was South Africa's minister of native affairs in the 1950s, instituted a number of policies that strictly regulated the lives of black citizens.

Satyagraha: The Force of Truth

The Indian community suffered discrimination in South Africa. Initially, Indian laborers had been brought to South Africa by the British to work on their sugarcane plantations of Natal. They were paid very little and their living and working conditions were bad. There were also a small number of Indian merchants who traveled to South Africa at their own expense and set up shop. In 1913, the government, alarmed at the number of Indians living in South Africa, passed the Immigration Bill to prevent further Indian immigration. Indians were not permitted to enter the Orange Free State and were prevented from purchasing land in the Transvaal.

Mohandas Gandhi.

In May 1893, Indian-born, London-educated Mohandas Karamchand Gandhi (who would become known as the *Mahatma*, or "great soul") went to South Africa to practice law. In Durban, he bought a first-class railway ticket and took his seat in a coach. During the journey, a white passenger objected to sharing his compartment with an Indian. Gandhi was thrown off the train after refusing to move to a third-class compartment. He referred to this incident as "the most important factor" in determining his future political life.

Gandhi became a key figure in campaigns for Indian rights. He started an Indian newspaper and a self-help settlement near Durban. As the government passed more and more restrictive laws to keep Indians down, Gandhi responded with a policy of passive resistance—letter writing campaigns, petitions, and protest marches. Instead of violence, Gandhi chose to use *satyagraha,* an Indian word meaning the "force of truth." He was arrested many times in his efforts to draw attention to the grievances of the Indian community.

In 1914, Gandhi returned to India, where he led the movement to win India's independence from Britain. His philosophy of nonviolent reform affected people all over the world. Gandhi was the inspiration for the peaceful defiance campaign in South Africa in 1952, which brought international attention to the plight of South Africa's Indian community.

Coloured People's Organisation, and the South African Congress of Democrats—the members of which were white—gathered to unite "all democratic elements around a common program," and to consider joint action. Its most lasting contribution was the Freedom Charter, a document expressing the democratic aspirations of the majority in South Africa. It included the following aims: that all national (race) groups should have equal rights; that land should be shared among those who work it; and that there should be a guarantee of work, security, and education for all.

A group of white South Africans gathered near Johannesburg in 1951 to protest government policies that had taken the vote away from blacks.

In December 1956, a security sweep led to the arrest of 156 anti-apartheid activists and supporters of the Freedom Charter. Their trial, named the "Treason Trial" after the charge brought against them, dragged on until 1961. Most of those who were charged were subsequently freed, or acquitted.

In 1959, unhappy with the ANC's ties with white liberals, Robert Sobukwe broke away from the group to form the Pan-Africanist Congress (PAC). In 1960, it organized a campaign of peaceful protest against the existing Pass Book laws, which involved demonstrations. The government's security forces reacted, killing sixty-nine

The Treason Trial, which lasted from 1956 to 1961, was an attempt by the government to silence some of the country's most influential anti-apartheid activists. Among the 156 people who were arrested was Nelson Mandela, standing tall in the third row in this group shot of the accused.

At Sharpeville in 1960, a peaceful protest turned violent when government forces opened fire on black marchers, killing sixty-nine people.

people at Sharpeville, a black township south of Johannesburg. A few days later 30,000 PAC supporters marched on a police station in Cape Town inviting arrest for being without their Pass Books. Riots erupted and the government reacted by clamping down stronger than ever. Strikes were swiftly and brutally broken. The ANC and the PAC were banned and forced underground.

At a secret ANC meeting in 1961, Nelson Mandela argued that the time had come for Africans to go over to armed struggle. *Umkhonto we Sizwe* (Spear of the Nation) was formed as the armed wing of the ANC's struggle against apartheid. At first, *Umkhonto* (pronounced OOM-kon-toe) concentrated on economic sabotage and political targets, attempting to avoid hurting people. Mandela slipped out of the country and began preparations for guerilla warfare before secretly returning to South Africa.

The PAC's *Poqo* (Standing Alone) movement began as a disorganized militant band with loose ties to leader Robert Sobukwe. *Poqo* (pronounced POE-coe) members planned and committed some terrorist acts. But, the police intercepted PAC messages to members regarding a general uprising, and their recipients were arrested.

The police detained, interrogated, and tortured hundreds of people. Activists from many different resistance groups were arrested and charged with sabotage.

In August 1962, eighteen Umkhonto leaders, including Mandela, were arrested in a raid on a Rivonia farmhouse outside Johannesburg. The secret police had been tipped off by an informer that a violent plan to overthrow the government was being created there. The Rivonia Trial lasted until mid-1964 and most of the leaders were found guilty of treason and sentenced to life imprisonment on Robben Island, an area that was used for political prisoners. Mandela spent more than a quarter of a century in prison while the world, and most South Africans, constantly clamored for his release.

Nelson Mandela, shown here in the early 1960s, before the Rivonia Trial and his subsequent imprisonment.

The Republic of South Africa

Meanwhile, South Africa had become a republic on May 31, 1961. Two months prior to that date, Prime Minister Verwoerd attended a Commonwealth Conference in London at which South Africa's policies came under severe attack from the other Commonwealth countries (former British colonies). In addition, a U.S. resolution at the United Nations called on members to consider what action they might take to bring about an end to apartheid. Verwoerd then withdrew South Africa's application to remain a part of the Commonwealth. He wanted to avoid interference in South Africa's internal affairs.

In the decade that followed, criticism of apartheid continued to mount while the government tried to convince the world that the establishment of independent homelands for the various racial groups in South Africa was the best solution to the country's problems. In 1970, the Bantu Homelands Citizenship Act was passed and enforced homeland boundaries that had been initially set up in the early 1950s. Blacks had been assigned to homelands in 1961. This law officially compelled blacks to become citizens of one of the homelands, regardless of whether or not they had ever lived there. Millions of blacks who were second- or third-generation city dwellers, and who had no connection to a tribal homeland, had to relocate. This act led to a series of forced removals of Africans from their subsequent resettlement.

In the 1974 all-white elections, the National Party won overwhelmingly again, but the liberal Progressive party did manage to win seven seats. This suggested that white opposition to apartheid was expanding.

The Soweto Riots and Repercussions

On Wednesday, June 16, 1976, thousands of black schoolchildren gathered in the sprawling black township of Soweto, just outside Johannesburg, to launch a peaceful protest against the inferior education they had been receiving. In particular, they objected to having to take half their high school classes in Afrikaans, the language of their oppressors. Their other classes were taught either in English, or a tribal language.

As they marched waving protest placards and singing freedom songs, the police and army arrived in force. In

Black Consciousness: Steve Bantu Biko

Following the banning of the ANC and the PAC, black students looked increasingly to the multiracial National Union of South African Students (NUSAS) as a vehicle to express their political aspirations.

However, NUSAS proved inadequate and, in 1967, a group of black students began to seriously analyze its options. The main force in this group was a young Natal University medical student named Steve Biko. He suggested an all-black university movement and, in 1969, the South African Students' Organisation (SASO) was formed with Biko as president.

In 1970, Biko launched an attack on the white liberal way of thinking. He felt that a true liberal educated other whites in preparing them to accept the future of majority rule, when blacks would have the vote. Biko wanted blacks to liberate themselves without a white leadership.

This "black consciousness" spawned a number of groups that were also influenced by the black theology and Black Power movements in the United States. By 1972, the Black Peoples' Convention had been set up as an umbrella organization for these groups.

In 1977, black consciousness groups were devastated when in September, Steve Biko was arrested for being a powerful anti-government leader, and died after being tortured in police detention.

In October, the minister of justice banned seventeen organizations and two newspapers, all of which he claimed had openly supported black consciousness.

In this photo, a police officer confronts demonstrators who have overturned a car during the violent aftermath of the Soweto protest.

response to tear gas attacks, the students threw stones at the police. Then the police opened fire on the unarmed children, killing 176 people. The effects of this tragedy were felt throughout the country and the rest of the world for a long time.

News of the children's deaths spread rapidly. Raging mobs of blacks set fire to government offices and vehicles in Soweto. Schools were closed and army and police anti-riot units were sent in. The violence spread to other parts of South Africa. In the aftermath, hundreds of people were killed—either in clashes with police or in clashes between rival black groups. In addition, thousands of people were arrested or detained without trial. Under the Terrorism Act, the police did not have to release information about those held.

For the remainder of 1976, and for a long time after, clashes between police and pupils, the burning of schools, and the mass detentions of suspected activists became a regular part of the black experience.

The Soweto uprisings brought forth a generation of youth who believed in their own power to change their lives. In the months that followed, hundreds of students and young citizens slipped across the border to join the ANC (and PAC, though it was in disarray). Since the ANC had been banned in South Africa since 1960, it had set up camps in neighboring countries. Trained and armed with AK-47 machine guns, explosives, and hand grenades, the first groups of the class of '76 began slipping back into the country. To some they were freedom fighters, to others they were terrorists.

An entire generation of children grew up unable to read and write because of ongoing school boycotts. Many of their schools had been damaged or destroyed during the riots. Political groups drafted children for their youth brigades. Almost every township child gave his or her allegiance to the ANC, PAC (both of which were banned organizations), Inkatha, or other parties.

Children raised in an atmosphere of political violence, with the constant hair-trigger police presence in their midst, had no qualms about killing people or destroying property in the name of the freedom struggle.

The great fear among moderate South Africans as they approached the 1994 elections was that these people, now unskilled, illiterate adults, would constitute a large section of the electorate. Many wondered who this generation would vote for and what place they would be offered in the new South Africa.

Intrigue and Fear

After the bloody Soweto riots, the situation in South Africa became increasingly complex. During this period, the government was determined to try to bolster the image of apartheid both at home and overseas. In an attempt to hold onto as much power for as long as possible, it adopted a strategy aimed at creating a black middle class as a counter to internal unrest. The government gave loans to some small black businesses and a few scholarships to black students. It also formed trade relationships with neighboring states and gave them financial aid in exchange for access to destroy bases in those countries.

In 1978, Prime Minister John Vorster was succeeded by P. W. Botha, who claimed to have a new program of reform to deal with the country's problems. These problems included the beginning of international sanctions that caused a deep economic slump, and increased black opposition, strikes, and boycotts.

Under Botha, notorious for telling whites to "adapt or die," South Africa made surface changes, while promising the rest of the world that apartheid would be dismantled. He scrapped many of the more blatant petty, or insubstantial, apartheid laws. Some discriminatory signs began to disappear from public places, leading eventually to concessions such as the repeal of the Mixed Marriages Act, and of laws prohibiting sex between blacks and whites in 1985, and the repeal of the Pass Book laws in 1986. However, at every step of the way, right-wing whites screamed that he was giving away too much, and anti-apartheid adherents cried that it was too little, too late.

Botha seemed to be taking two steps forward, and one step back in 1983, when he announced that a Tricameral (three-chamber) Parliament would be established. This meant that coloreds and Indians would be represented. Some issues would be voted on jointly, others separately. Blacks were still excluded. Opposition to the Tricameral Parliament by all anti-apartheid South Africans was overwhelming.

Allan Boesak, a prominent black (classified as colored) leader, disgusted at the exclusion of the entire African population, was instrumental in founding the United Democratic Front (UDF). The movement was supported by Archbishop Desmond Tutu, leader of the Anglican Church in South Africa.

The UDF was an umbrella movement that united more than 500 organizations in a nonracial front against apartheid. The government hurried to suppress the UDF, and within a year, forty-five of its eighty leaders were in jail.

Around the same time, the National Forum (NF) was inaugurated. Its vision of a future South Africa was different from the UDF's. The NF wanted a revolutionary

Allan Boesak helped to found the United Democratic Front (UDF), which was a broad-based coalition that united hundreds of organizations against apartheid.

campaign to restructure society completely by overthrowing the "racist/capitalist" order. Violent clashes between certain groups under the UDF umbrella and NF supporters threatened to turn into a civil war and black-on-black violence ran rampant.

Since 1986, supporters of some UDF groups have engaged in one bloody clash after another with Chief Buthelezi's movement, Inkatha. Buthelezi's KwaZulu (a Zulu homeland in the Natal province) police force has been accused of fostering violence between rival black groups, and the South African government has been suspected of funding some of these hit squads. It was long a covert policy of the South African government to encourage tribal and political disunity among various African groups, so as to maintain white supremacy. Tragically, thousands of people have been killed, injured, or made homeless through black-on-black violence.

By 1985, the parts of South Africa that were inhabited mostly by whites gave the outward appearance of being quiet, controlled, and secure. People surrounded their homes with high walls and installed high-tech burglar alarms to keep out the rising tide of crime. In the "other" South Africa, school boycotts continued because education for blacks was still unequal; and unemployment, mass stayaways (when people "stay away" from work), and strikes were common. Poverty and violence were the order of the day. Police and army vehicles patrolled the troubled township streets.

In July 1985, the security situation became so bad that President Botha imposed a state of emergency. This greatly increased the government's powers to detain anyone who was suspected of fomenting violence. Organized political meetings were banned. But the violence did not stop. A second, more stringent, emergency was imposed in 1986, with strict censorship of the media. Any activity that even hinted at opposition to the government was crushed. But the violence was still not quelled.

Zulu Chief Mangosuthu Buthelezi founded Inkatha, a black nationalist movement that gained power in South Africa in the late 1980s.

Members of Inkatha demonstrate in downtown Johannesburg. Clashes between Inkatha and other groups weakened unity among blacks in the country.

With the threat of international sanctions held over it, the government began entertaining the first ideas about power-sharing with blacks, before the whole system unraveled completely. The reaction was a divided country that began to splinter even farther.

Chapter 4

Dismantling Apartheid

Change was inevitable; it was just a matter of how and when it would happen. The elaborate network of discriminatory laws that comprised apartheid began to unravel. Internal troubles wracked the country. External pressure held it in a viselike grip.

International Pressure

Since its inception in 1948, many people all over the world have been opposed to apartheid. These people began to employ a number of ways to persuade South Africa's leaders to change their ways. Sanctions and embargoes, often the most effective because they directly affect the economy of the country, were among the first tactics to be used.

In 1968, various African countries threatened to boycott the Mexico Olympics if South Africa took part. South Africa was excluded, and was expelled altogether from the Olympic Games in 1970. Ultimately, any country that maintained sporting links with South Africa risked isolation from the international sports community. (But slowly, interracial sports have returned in South Africa, and

> By 1990, it was clear that the civil rights of South Africa's black citizens could no longer be denied

Opposite:
Thousands of ANC supporters celebrate in 1990 upon hearing the news that Nelson Mandela would be released from prison after twenty-six years of confinement.

Ending Apartheid: A Political and Cultural Issue in the United States

On many college campuses across the United States in the mid-1980s, you could find replicas of black South African shanty towns. Close by, would be an information board or a table set up to explain that the students had made the shanty towns to protest their schools' South African investments, and to demand their withdrawal, or divestment. Often students demanded their universities not do business with any company having ties to South Africa. Other tactics were also used. In 1987, for example, the graduating class of Oberlin College in Ohio, invited Bishop Tutu to be the graduation speaker. He accepted and, by May 1987, Oberlin College had divested.

The issue of divestment was frequently debated in schools and around boardroom tables of U.S. businesses. Letter-writing campaigns and petitions attracted the attention of politicians, who were also being pressured by civil rights groups to push for more sweeping sanctions against South Africa. Lobbyists and students worked hard and eventually were successful.

acceptance back into the Olympics in 1992 was the reward for significant political reforms made by the government.)

Famous international entertainers also weighed the risks versus the benefits of playing to segregated audiences in South Africa. A South African appearance could seriously damage a performer's reputation and he or she might be ostracized by the entertainment industry.

These measures were frustrating to South Africans who supported apartheid, but did nothing to bring about real change. It seemed the only way to force the end of apartheid was by crippling the South African economy. But this was not so simple. Many European and U.S. companies and individuals had millions of dollars invested in South African business and industry. They wanted to protect their investments. Some did not want to forego profits or lose money. Others were concerned that by divesting, they would leave behind massive unemployment, thereby hurting the blacks whom they had intended to help.

The British in 1974, followed by the Americans in 1976, did begin to address the issue of persuading the government, through business, to abandon its apartheid policies. British companies operating in South Africa were to follow a "code of practice" pressing for African job advancement, an end to wage and other workplace discrimination, and the recognition of African trade unions.

Reverend Leon Sullivan, a vocal American civil rights worker, at first called on U.S. companies to withdraw from South Africa. When they refused, he then proposed the Sullivan code of principles urging U.S. firms to remove discrimination from their factories and offices in South Africa.

The European Economic Community (an organization of western European countries that was established for mutual trading benefits) asked European companies doing business in South Africa to recognize unions and institute various reforms. These codes were precursors to a new wave of international sanctions that would come particularly as a result of political lobbying in the United States.

America and Divestment

As the ANC's influence grew internationally, its call for sanctions was taken more seriously. The ANC felt that sanctions were the best way to gain world support and that this method would mainly hurt those who were profiting financially under apartheid. An extreme problem required an extreme solution. More voices joined the call to economic action.

The involvement of the United States in South Africa was complicated. The Republican Reagan administration pursued a policy of "constructive engagement" with South Africa whereby sanctions were not actively encouraged. Meanwhile the Democrats pushed a sanctions package through the Senate in 1986. New investments and loans to South Africa were stopped, landing rights for South African Airways were withdrawn, and a long list of imports from South Africa were banned. Soon after, huge companies like General Electric, IBM, and Coca-Cola closed down their South African operations.

During the 1980s and 1990s, Archbishop Desmond Tutu became an influential international voice against apartheid—in favor of economic sanctions against South Africa. Here, he speaks in favor of divestment at a graduation at Oberlin College in May 1987.

People who supported sanctions in the United States argued that these measures would bring a peaceful end to the unrest. ANC leaders said that so many people were already living in poverty with few rights, that they were prepared to make the sacrifice to bring an end to apartheid. Sanctions would only truly hurt those who had something to lose in the first place. After years of opposing sanctions, Archbishop Tutu became a convincing spokesman for divestment, declaring, "When the ladder falls, it is those at the top who get hurt most." Tutu saw no alternative to sanctions, and explained his reasoning on the international lecture circuit. Tutu also united a number of anti-apartheid groups in a peaceful forum in which they could work towards bringing justice and equality to all South Africans. When he received the Nobel Peace Prize in 1984, he was given even greater credibility and a huge captive audience.

Calls for sanctions came from the Commonwealth. Only British prime minister Margaret Thatcher held out against severe economic action. Limited sanctions were also imposed by the European Economic Community, including a ban on the sales of South African gold coins, called Krugerrands. Sweden and Denmark opted for a total trade ban.

The Pressures Within

In 1989, one expert estimated that only 10 percent of the South African population supported apartheid. The South African economy was ailing. The cost of keeping apartheid alive was enormous. So much money was spent on creating and enforcing the system that there was little left over for health care, education, and job creation. With the application of sanctions, inflation and unemployment skyrocketed. This had severe consequences for the already weakened stability of the country.

In the elections of September 1989, the National Party lost votes to both the left and the right, but came to power once again with F. W. de Klerk as president. The Conservative party and the Democratic party gained many new seats in Parliament. These were to be the last elections from which blacks would be excluded. The internal pressures for total reform were so overwhelming that the only alternative to getting rid of apartheid would have been full-scale civil war. So real change was promised, and real change was begun.

In February 1990, de Klerk lifted the ban on the African National Congress (ANC) and the South African Communist party. The world's most famous political prisoner, Nelson Mandela, was released. Other political prisoners were also released, and banned activists like Joe Slovo, a white lawyer who was a leader of the South African Communist party, returned from exile to participate in negotiations for democracy.

To this end, President de Klerk called for a referendum in March 1992 asking the white electorate to respond as to whether or not he continue on the road to real democracy. The response was a vote of confidence in both the president and his policy to end apartheid.

In August 1990, the decision by Nelson Mandela and the ANC to suspend its armed struggle marked the turning point in the transition from violent conflict to peaceful negotiation.

The release of Nelson Mandela from prison in 1990 signaled the beginning of a new era in South African politics. Upon his release, Mandela mobilized the ANC to step up efforts to end apartheid.

In July 1991, the government reached a difficult compromise on the principle of an interim government and a constituent assembly—a fully represented multi-racial Parliament. Although many whites began to accept the inevitability of majority rule and had voted for a change in the March 1992 referendum, they would not simply hand over power all at once. They feared sudden change would lead to chaos and bloodshed. An intricate system had to be developed whereby power sharing would lead to full majority rule.

The road to reform was not smooth. There was growing concern about persistent violence among blacks, increasing militancy and terrorist actions by right-wing whites, economic stagnation, and rampant crime that knew no racial barriers. Just as negotiations were getting underway, the government's position was weakened by its part in the June 1992 Boipatong massacre. This was an outbreak of violence in a township between the ANC and the IFP. Police were called in and sided with the IFP, against the ANC. The international community was again drawn into the fray. The United Nations Security Council debated the situation and sent a special envoy to South Africa to help.

Strides forward were being offset by steps backward. However, the big picture clearly showed the nation moving toward the total dismantling of apartheid.

The massacre at Boipatong in 1992 left many dead and increased tensions between the ANC and the government during their negotiating process.

Chapter 5

Voting for a New Future

By 1991, the countdown to democracy had clearly begun. In some ways, the negotiations between the Nationalist government and the ANC really began while Nelson Mandela was still sitting in his prison cell. Now, in a whirlwind of change, Mandela seemed poised to be the first black president of South Africa. But even so, many problems lay ahead.

The Transitional Executive Council (TEC) had its first meeting on December 7, 1993. The TEC was composed of representatives from the ANC, the white government, and fourteen other black and white groups. It had significant powers and served as a watchdog before the elections. Mandela described the seating of the council as "a victory for all the people of South Africa, without exception."

The irreversible process was under way. A new constitution was drafted with extreme care. But while this happened, extremist splinter groups were doing all they could to hinder the process.

Who Sat at the Negotiating Table?

The first meeting of the Convention for a Democratic South Africa (CODESA) took place in Johannesburg in December 1991. These were the first actual negotiations

In 1994, South Africa scheduled a vote in which every citizen, regardless of race, would cast a ballot

Opposite:
In February 1990, South Africans in Soweto celebrated as they listened to Nelson Mandela advocate the right of every citizen to participate in the voting process.

over a transition of power. (Everything prior had been talks about talks.) CODESA was possible because many groups chose to join the process. The largest groups involved at that stage were the National Party/government, the ANC, and the IFP.

In the violent and tumultuous period between June and September of 1992, CODESA realized that there had to be a pact between the government and the ANC to support their contest for political power. In addition, a decision was made that the negotiations could not continue being disrupted by political violence. The process had to go on regardless.

The NP and the ANC were at the negotiating table from the start. Buthelezi's IFP was there at the beginning, then vowed to boycott the elections, but returned to negotiations. The following parties were also a part of CODESA negotiations: the PAC, the Conservative party, the Democratic party, and various others. There were nineteen groups involved in negotiations and they represented the full spectrum of political persuasions.

Preparing for Change

South Africans and the international community began preparing for the transition of power. Newspapers and television programs offered voter education in a fun and interesting way, using cartoons and diagrams. Colorful posters and billboards displayed information about the significance of the elections. Catchy jingles played on the radio in many of South Africa's diverse languages. For the first time, it was vital that all population groups understand the election process so that they could play a role in South Africa's future.

Voter education resources distributed a sample ballot paper to show people who had never voted before exactly how to do it. The sample ballot paper listed seventeen political parties with a fine print disclaimer at the bottom,

South African president F. W. de Klerk (left), ANC president Nelson Mandela, and Inkatha leader Mangosuthu Buthelezi sit together during negotiations in 1992.

explaining that some of those listed may choose not to enter the elections.

Meanwhile, the world watched. It was ready to welcome South Africa back into the family of nations. Steps taken toward democracy were being rewarded. The era of sanctions drew to a close.

Herman J. Cohen, assistant secretary for African affairs during the Bush administration, made a statement to the House Foreign Affairs Committee on March 31, 1992, announcing that South Africa had made "significant progress" in eliminating apartheid. He said that loans could again be made available and that a team would be sent to explore the investment climate with the South African government and other parties engaged in the CODESA process. The U.S. Agency for International Development announced a $30 million housing project for victims of apartheid. In conclusion, the United States expressed its concern that the international community support South Africa during this crucial period.

By late 1993, virtually all remaining sanctions were lifted to enable the new democratic country to rebuild and become financially stable. This way, the transition was more likely to be peaceful.

Roadblocks to Democracy

As election day drew closer, optimism over the prospect of change combined with fear for many people. Some who foresaw an ANC victory attempted to sabotage that eventuality.

Acts of terrorism wrenched the country. Chris Hani, leader of the ANC's military wing, was assassinated by white anti-Communists in 1993. Members of the white supremacist Afrikaner Resistance Movement violently disrupted the first election planning meeting at Johannesburg's World Trade Center in July 1993.

White extremists affiliated with several groups threatened order all the way up to election eve. On April 24, 1994, just days before voters went to the polls, a car bomb exploded in downtown Johannesburg, killing nine people. The next day, more than a dozen explosions rocked various parts of the country. Many were minor but the worst ripped through a taxi stand outside Johannesburg, killing ten blacks. Believing the blasts to be the work of white extremists, police acted quickly and by April 27, arrested thirty-one suspects.

The specter of violence between the IFP and ANC also haunted the nation in the home stretch toward the elections. In January 1994, gunmen in the IFP-dominated

Neo-Nazis: A Fight to the Death

The Afrikaner Weerstandsbeweging (AWB) or Afrikaner Resistance Movement is a group of militant white supremacists led by the charismatic, gun-toting Eugene Terre'Blanche. Terre'Blanche is a white miner who worked stockpiling weapons and dynamite. Precise membership figures for the AWB are kept secret. Entire families belong to the movement and attend camps from time to time where speeches are made designed to whip up their enthusiasm for their cause. The children dress in uniforms similar to those worn by Hitler Youth in Germany at the time of World War II.

Members of the AWB have threatened to carry out acts of sabotage to put obstacles in the way of a democratic, integrated South Africa. They forced their way into an election-planning meeting in July 1993, in an attempt to disrupt negotiations. In December 1993, a black commuter train was derailed by explosives suspected to have been placed by white supremacists. They are violently opposed to racial integration and would rather secede from their country than be a part of it. Their other option is to fight to the death. This they have sworn to do.

Members of the Afrikaner Weerstandsbeweging (AWB).

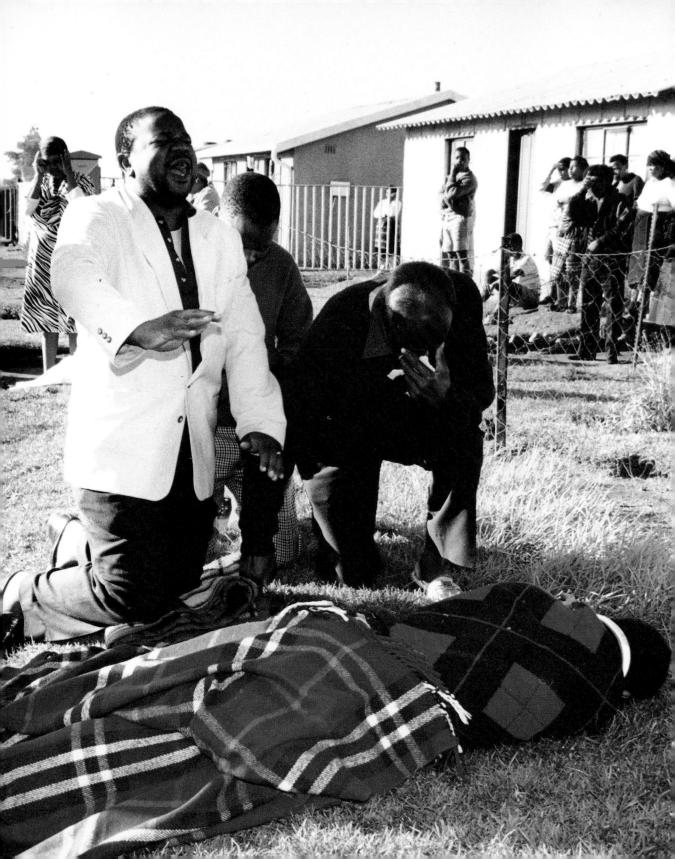

Katlehong township opened fire on ANC supporters including ANC Secretary General Cyril Ramaphosa and Communist party leader Joe Slovo. Although Ramaphosa and Slovo were uninjured, one journalist was killed and several people were wounded.

Only weeks before the vote, IFP chief Buthelezi withdrew his party from the ballot. The black homeland over which Buthelezi ruled, like all black homelands created under apartheid, was to be abolished by the new government. Fearing he would be left powerless, Buthelezi said he would not participate in the elections without a guarantee of autonomy for his region. Meanwhile, some of Buthelezi's well-armed followers vowed an all-out war on a victorious ANC. The possibility of large-scale violence between the ANC and IFP made citizens of all colors uneasy. The black townships of Natal, the IFP's home province, erupted in violence that became so serious that

Opposite:
Violence claimed a number of lives following the assassination of black ANC military leader Chris Hani in 1993.

As negotiations took place inside the Johannesburg World Trade Center in 1993, thousands of South Africans protested outside. This man, in traditional dress, was marching with demonstrators who wanted strong workers' rights in the new constitution.

de Klerk's waning white government declared a state of emergency there. Everyone breathed a sigh of relief when Buthelezi, perhaps seeing that South Africa's move toward an ANC-dominated democratic future was irreversible, returned to the ballot in April.

At the Crossroads

These roadblocks to democracy, however, could not stop this nation at the crossroads from moving forward. From April 26 to April 29, 1994, 22 million South Africans went to the polls. Over 17 million of them were blacks who were choosing their leaders for the first time. (South Africans living abroad were allowed to participate in the

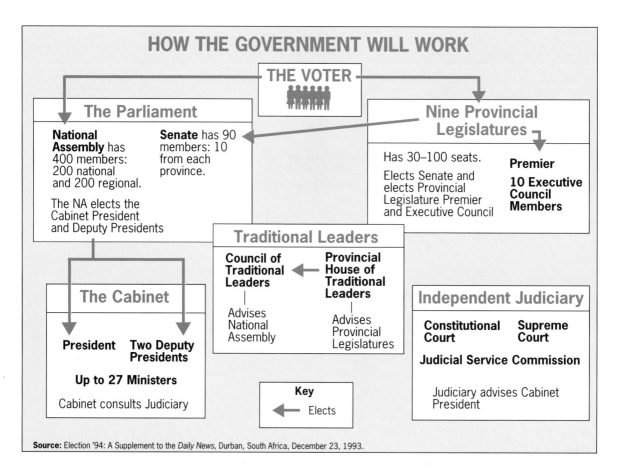

HOW THE GOVERNMENT WILL WORK

THE VOTER

The Parliament

National Assembly has 400 members: 200 national and 200 regional.

The NA elects the Cabinet President and Deputy Presidents

Senate has 90 members: 10 from each province.

Nine Provincial Legislatures

Has 30–100 seats.

Elects Senate and elects Provincial Legislature Premier and Executive Council

Premier

10 Executive Council Members

Traditional Leaders

Council of Traditional Leaders
|
Advises National Assembly

Provincial House of Traditional Leaders
|
Advises Provincial Legislatures

The Cabinet

President   **Two Deputy Presidents**

Up to 27 Ministers

Cabinet consults Judiciary

Independent Judiciary

Constitutional Court   **Supreme Court**

Judicial Service Commission

Judiciary advises Cabinet President

Key

← Elects

Source: Election '94: A Supplement to the *Daily News*, Durban, South Africa, December 23, 1993.

elections, and some 130,000 South Africans in the U.S. voted.)

The first day of voting was reserved for the elderly and disabled and for prisoners and soldiers. Blacks in their seventies and eighties, who had lived many of those years under apartheid, came to the polls, sometimes supported by the arms of younger generations. Voters arrived in wheelchairs and on crutches, and death row inmates cast ballots that were literally a matter of life and death: The ANC vowed to do away with capital punishment.

The remainder of South Africans voted next. Lines at some polling places stretched for miles, and for many voting was an all-day affair. It quickly became obvious that the white government's census had underestimated the numbers of blacks in many areas: Polling stations ran out of ballots and a day (April 29) had to be added to accommodate the extra voters.

Despite these problems and charges of tampering in some locations, the elections proceeded with relative calm. As Nelson Mandela, who cast his ballot at a schoolhouse in Natal province, remarked: "We are starting a new era of hope, of reconciliation, of nation-building."

The New Constitution and Government

An important step in nation-building came on April 28, when the country's new constitution took effect. The forerunner of a permanent constitution that the new government would write within five years, the document guaranteed the elimination of apartheid. It also had a Bill of Fundamental Rights providing equal treatment under the law for everyone, regardless of race, religion, or sex.

The constitution also outlined the structure of the new government for which citizens were choosing leaders. South Africa would have both a federal government consisting of a parliament and cabinet and nine provincial governments. (These were created from the councils of

Before the 1994 vote, many black South Africans participated in classes and other programs that helped to prepare new voters to use their hard-fought new right.

the country's provinces.) Each voter selected a party (not a specific candidate) for the parliament and provincial legislatures. These, in turn, were responsible for appointing a cabinet that included the country's president and a senate.

Even before vote counting commenced, Mandela began laying out his party's plans for governing. The new government, Mandela vowed, would be based on consensus: Members of the white government who won seats in the parliament would be accepted as legitimate partners. Mandela indicated that even members of extremist groups who did not win the right to participate in the government would be somehow included. Beyond compromise, however, was the ANC's social program. Intended to correct the injustices blacks suffered under apartheid, the program called for building one million houses within five years, creating jobs, and guaranteeing free education.

'I Am Your Servant'

By May 2, the tallying showed that the vast majority of South Africans had called upon the ANC to lead them into the future. On national television, the party's graying representative responded humbly: "I am your servant."

That night black South Africans rode a wave of pure joy. They poured into the streets, dancing and singing: "We are free at last." Mobs in one black township blocked a white driver's way. Instead of harming the man, they circled his car in celebration. His reaction seemed to reflect that of many whites: "This all can be scary. But it's great, too, isn't it?"

Early returns showed the National Party trailing the ANC with approximately 23 percent of the vote, followed by the IFP with 5 percent. This allowed de Klerk to become one of two vice presidents and Buthelezi to take a seat in the cabinet.

In an eloquent concession speech, de Klerk said: "Mr. Mandela has walked a long road, and now stands at the top of the hill. A traveler would sit down and admire the view. But a man of destiny knows that beyond this hill lies another and another. The journey is never complete."

Aware that South Africa's greatest challenges may still be yet to come, Nelson Mandela said in his victory speech: "Let our celebrations be in keeping with the mood set in the elections, peaceful, respectful and disciplined, showing we are a people ready to assume the responsibilities of government."

Little more than a week later, on May 10, Nelson Mandela was scheduled to make history by assuming those responsibilities of South Africa's first black leader.

Chronology

Pre-Iron Age	San hunter-gatherers, then Khoikhoi herdsmen, inhabit southern Africa.
AD 300	Bantu-speaking black herders migrate to southern Africa.
1652	Jan van Riebeeck sets up refreshment station at the Cape for the Dutch East India Company. Dutch settlement begins at the southern tip of Africa.
1795	First British occupation of the Cape.
1806	Second British occupation. British way of life becomes dominant over Dutch/Boer way of life.
1820	First major influx of British settlers to the eastern Cape.
1833	Emancipation of slaves in all British colonies, including the Cape.
1836	Start of the Great Trek. Boers travel inland to found their own republic away from British domination.
1841	Britain annexes Natal.
1854	Southern Africa is divided into two Boer republics— Orange Free State and the Transvaal.
1860	First Indian immigrants arrive in Natal.
1867	First diamond discovered in Griqualand West.
1880	Transvaal Boers rise up against British.
1886	Discovery of gold on the Witwatersrand and foundation of Johannesburg.
1899–1902	Anglo-Boer War.
1902	Treaty of Vereeniging. Transvaal and the Orange Free State become British colonies (in addition to existing colonies of the Cape and Natal).
1906	Gandhi leads a passive resistance campaign against pass laws for Indians.
1908–1909	Meeting of all-white National Convention.
1909	Meeting of black South African Native Convention delegation fails to persuade the British government to extend voting rights to blacks.
1910	Formation of the Union of South Africa.
1912	Delegates of the Native Convention form the African National Native Congress, later known as the African National Congress (ANC).
1914-1918	South Africa fights on the side of Britain against Germany in World War I.
1920	Native Affairs Act sets up tribally based, government appointed district councils.
1936	Prime Minister Hertzog passes Native Representation Act putting blacks in the Cape on a separate voters roll.
1939–1945	The country is divided before deciding to fight in World War II on the side of Britain and the Allies.
1948	D. F. Malan and the National Party win whites-only election. Apartheid begins.
Early 1950's	Beginning of laws to enforce apartheid.
1952	Members of the ANC and South African Indian Congress (SAIC) begin

	defiance campaign, risking arrest to deliberately break segregation laws.
1955	The Freedom Charter is written, expressing democratic desires of South Africans.
1956–1961	Treason Trial for anti-apartheid activists.
1960	Sharpeville Massacre. Police fire on peaceful protesters. Officially, sixty-nine killed.
May 31, 1961	South Africa resigns from the Commonwealth and becomes a republic.
Early 1960's	Mandela and others arrested and tried during Rivonia Trial. ANC and PAC banned. Mandela convicted and sentenced to life imprisonment.
1970	The Bantu Homelands Citizenship Act is passed.
June 16, 1976	Soweto Riots begin.
1980's	Urban terrorism by militant anti-apartheid groups increases. Early sanctions begin. Some petty apartheid laws are repealed.
1983	Tricameral Parliament represents whites, coloreds, and Indians. Blacks excluded.
1984	Archbishop Desmond Tutu wins Nobel Peace Prize.
July 1985	Prime Minister Botha imposes a state of emergency as violence increases.
1986	A second, stricter state of emergency is imposed to quell political violence.
February 1990	President F. W. de Klerk legalizes the ANC and the SACP. Nelson Mandela released from prison.
August 1990	ANC announces suspension of armed struggle.
December 1991	Convention for a Democratic South Africa meets for discussions.
March 1992	Bush administration announces that "significant progress" is being made in eliminating apartheid.
April 1993	Chris Hani assassinated by white anti-Communists.
July 1993	AWB disrupts CODESA negotiations. St. James' Church massacre.
Fall 1993	Amy Biehl killed in Cape Town by APLA.
November 18, 1993	New constitution endorsed.
December 1993	Shared Nobel Peace Prize awarded to Nelson Mandela and President de Klerk.
March 1994	Mangosuthu Buthelezi withdraws from the ballot. His followers vow violence against the ANC. A state of emergency is declared in Natal. Buthelezi subsequently returns to the elections.
April 24–25, 1994	A series of bombs explode in Johannesburg and throughout South Africa as part of a terror campaign launched by white extremists. Thirty-one suspects are later arrested in connection with the explosions.
April 26–29, 1994	South Africa holds its first all-race elections amidst an atmosphere of relative calm.
May 2, 1994	Nelson Mandela, representing the African National Congress, declares victory and is scheduled to become the nation's first black president.

For Further Reading

Brickhill, Joan. *South Africa: The End of Apartheid?* New York: Franklin Watts, 1991.

Cowell, Alan and Turnley, David. *Why Are They Weeping?* New York: Workman Publishing, 1988.

Hughes, Libby. *Nelson Mandela: Voice of Freedom.* New York: Macmillan Children's Book Group, 1992.

Otfinoski, Steven. *Nelson Mandela: The Fight Against Apartheid.* Brookfield, CT: Millbrook Press, 1992.

Pascoe, Elaine. *South Africa: Troubled Land.* Revised edition. New York: Franklin Watts, 1992,

Paton, Jonathan. *The Land and People of South Africa.* New York: J.B. Lippincott, 1990.

Smith, Chris. *Conflict in Southern Africa.* New York: Macmillan Children's Book Group, 1993.

Stein, R. Conrad. *South Africa.* Chicago: Childrens Press, 1986.

Index

Acknowledgements and photo credits

Cover: Hollyman/Gamma Liaison; p. 4: H. Marais-Barrit/Gamma Liaison; pp. 6, 23 (bottom), 28, 29, 30, 32, 35, 44: UPI/Bettmann; p. 8 : UPI/Bettmann Newsphotos; pp. 9, 10, 26, 37, 54: Reuters/Bettmann; p. 13: ©Drew Gardnee/Katz/SABA; p. 14: The Bettmann Archive; p. 18: North Wind Archives; pp. 20, 22, 23 (top): Culver Pictures, Inc.; p. 25: Bettmann; p. 31: Gamma Liaison; p. 33: Reuters/Bettmann Newsphotos; pp. 38, 51: ©South Light/Gamma Liaison; p. 39: ©Haviv/SABA; p. 40: Scott Peterson/Gamma Liaison; p. 46: Eric Bouvet/Gamma Liaison; p. 47: Mabuza Herbert/Gamma Liaison; p. 48: ©Ron Haviv/SABA; p. 53: ©Oosterbroeken/Gamma Liaison; p. 55: Wide World Photos, Inc.; p. 58: ©Peter Magubane/Gamma Liaison.
Maps by Blackbirch Graphics, Inc.